Dying well, Michael Mercer suggests, is about healing. Not physical healing, but soul work—emotional and spiritual healing that brings meaning to our final days and gives us the courage to let go. Hospice chaplain Mike Mercer reminds us that we need not make this final journey alone and that some of our best guides are those who have gone before us with grace.

☀ **BERYL SCHEWE**, *chaplain, pastoral care director, and author of* **Habits of Resilience: Learning to Live Fully in the Midst of Loss**

This is a thoughtfully written book. It offers a glimpse into the life of a hospice chaplain that yields important insights to help us on the "walk home." It is also reflective of one man's experience of truly listening—as Mike Mercer does.

☀ **DR. DALE THEOBALD, PHD, MD**, *Senior Medical Director for Community Home Health and Life's Journey, Indianapolis, IN*

Chaplain Mike takes your hand and walks on the last road of life with you with compassion, insight, and humor. There is more life here than in any other book on death.

☀ **JEFF DUNN**, *author of* **Why Worry? A Catholic's Guide For Learning To Let Go**

In our society, few people ever talk about death, which can leave those who have received a terminal diagnosis in an awkward position. In this book, hospice chaplain Mike Mercer addresses, with the wisdom of his years of experience, the fears and concerns of someone facing death. Simple but profound, the author's observations and stories are a source of great comfort.

☀ **DAMARIS ZEHNER**, *author of* **The Between Time: Savoring the Sacred Moments of Everyday Life**

*Walking Home Together* is a book on dying that will comfort, inspire, and even evoke a sense of anticipation. As a hospice chaplain, Mike Mercer has lived squarely in the most intimate moments of the dying and developed a wisdom and kindness to help talk us through our fears, work out concerns for loved ones, plan practicalities, and remind us that our last days are still full of life and can be an enduring gift to others. He shows us how to say goodbye with purpose.

☀ **LISA DYE**, *author of* **30 Days with 30 Saints**

WALKING HOME TOGETHER

Michael Mercer

# WALKING HOME TOGETHER

**SPIRITUAL GUIDANCE
& PRACTICAL ADVICE
FOR THE END OF LIFE**

TWENTY-THIRD
PUBLICATIONS
twentythirdpublications.com

**Twenty-Third Publications**

1 Montauk Avenue, Suite 200, New London, CT 06320

(860) 437-3012 » (800) 321-0411 » www.twentythirdpublications.com

ISBN: 978-1-62785-149-7
Library of Congress Catalog Card Number: 2015957205
Printed in the U.S.A.

# CONTENTS

# A good walk home

WHEN I WAS YOUNG, WE WALKED. IT SEEMS TO ME NOW THAT we walked everywhere. We walked to and from school. We walked to our friends' homes, and I distinctly remember walking to my grandparents' house on the other side of town. We walked to fields of dreams where we chose teams and played our games. We walked to the neighborhood store and plunked down our nickels and dimes to buy candy, pop, and baseball cards. We walked downtown, to church for choir practice after school, and to the pool in summer. We got to baseball practice by walking, and we carried basketballs under our arms as we walked to the courts at the park. We leaned fishing poles on our shoulders as we walked to the banks of the river just above the dam in hopes of catching some bullheads or catfish. We walked to the record store to pick up that week's Top 40 list and—when we had saved up enough—

to buy the latest 45. Sometimes we rode our bikes, but mostly we walked.

We walked on streets and sidewalks, through grassy fields and mown lawns. One childhood house where I lived was connected to the entire neighborhood by a string of backyards uninterrupted by fences or barriers of any kind (there were fewer fences then), and the neighbors kindly let us treat it as a thoroughfare and playground. We could walk up and down the brick street in front or through the yards in back and get most anywhere children would want to be.

As we got older, we continued to walk but with new companions. It was then that we walked the neighborhoods with girlfriends and boyfriends, in mixed groups of those who were going steady and those who hoped to be soon. As time went on, some escaped the group in pairs and walked as couples, exploring youthful dreams and timeless mysteries together.

A good deal of our walking in those days was aimless. We were just "walking around," we told our parents. But whether we went to a certain destination or not or for a particular purpose or not, eventually it came time for us to walk home. At some point we came back around; the walk was complete; we said goodbye and then bounded up the steps and through the screen door. We were home.

This book is about the walk home.

Whether simply on account of advanced age or through a terminal diagnosis you have received, you have reached a place in your life where you know you're on the way home. You are on the final leg of your life's journey. You will soon pass through a door called "death" and be home. Your home may be across town—a good long trek—or it could be a few streets away or perhaps just around the next corner. It may even be in sight, and in a few steps the door will beckon. Soon you will say goodbye to those with whom you've journeyed through life, go through that door we call "death," and enter another reality. You will be home.

My purpose in this book is to accompany you on this homeward portion of your walk. I would count it a privilege to be your companion, to help you think through what a "good walk home" might look like for you.

Henri Nouwen once wrote:

> Is death something so terrible and absurd that we are better off not thinking or talking about it? Is death such an undesirable part of our existence that we are better off acting as if it were not real? Is death such an absolute end of all our thoughts and actions that we simply cannot face it? Or is it possible to befriend our dying gradually and live open to it, trusting that we have nothing to fear? Is it possible to prepare for our death with the same attentiveness that our parents had in preparing for our birth? Can we wait for our death as for a friend who wants to welcome us home? ◁ **HENRI NOUWEN**, *Our Greatest Gift*

In my daily work, I serve as a hospice chaplain. I work with individuals and their families who find themselves at this stage of life.

The older I get, the more I discover that each of life's seasons has its own path, its own challenges, and its own rewards. The "end of life" season is no different, and I think it is important that we give it some attention since we are all going to have to make that journey.

Last summer, I went to visit my Uncle Bill. He was the comedian in our family, telling jokes to anyone who would listen, making funny remarks about everything going on around him, sending us gag gifts for birthdays and holidays. He loved life and lived large, and we enjoyed every moment we could be around him.

Bill was also transparent about struggles he had experienced in his life. He had a problem with alcohol for years. He smoked constantly. He loved to gamble. He'd had some difficult relationships. Whenever Bill talked about these things, he exposed a soft and vulnerable interior. Underneath his clown-like persona lay a thoughtful and sensitive heart.

Bill and his family had just been through an exhausting two-year ordeal with his wife, my aunt. She'd had a cerebrovascular event that left her confused and debilitated. She had gone through rehabilitation and stints in facilities, and there were times the family wondered if she would ever recover to any meaningful extent or whether she would make it out of this situation alive. Somehow, in what seemed like a miraculous revival, she came back and began doing activities like cooking, playing cards, walking, and even driving. Still, she had to be looked after and helped, and my uncle was becoming worn down.

Then, Bill, worn out and filled with worries about his wife, was diagnosed with lung cancer. The prognosis was not good. He called me one day and asked several questions about treatment and hospice care.

As he began to decline significantly, I decided I should pay my Uncle Bill a visit while he could still enjoy the company. I hoped to be an encouragement, but to be honest, this trip was for me too. I was feeling what we in hospice call "anticipatory grief." So I boarded a plane and flew out to spend a week with Bill and the family.

We had a wonderful time together. I took him to chemotherapy sessions and we had heart-to-heart talks about his life, his illness, what he'd been through with my aunt the past few years, his relationships, even his childhood and perspectives I had never heard before regarding our family. We shared memories and stories. I updated him on my life, my family, my work. We discussed his ideas about spirituality and religion.

Because Bill couldn't sleep at night, he would go across the highway to the casino in the wee hours, and I joined him on one of those outings. I even brought him a little beginner's luck! I helped with a few small tasks around the house, and he played the part of the strict supervisor, rightly criticizing my all-thumbs approach to getting the job done. Most of all, we laughed.

He was so thin and gaunt, but nothing could stop Bill's sense of humor. He continued smoking like a smokestack, going out to his truck so he wouldn't disturb anyone else. Mostly he sat in his chair, watching TV, dozing on and off, keeping a limited daily routine of activities.

What impressed me most about my Uncle Bill was that he had been and continued to be extremely diligent about making sure things would be in place for his wife and children when he died. Bill had a successful career with the phone company and did pretty well financially. He shared with me how he had arranged things to make sure his family would be secure in the future. He had taken care of what would happen with his house and assets. He had talked with his children about options for taking care of their mother. He even shared about steps he had taken to heal some difficult relationships.

Bill knew that he would soon be going home. His wife's health problems and now his own had awakened him to a sharp awareness that the final season of life was upon him.

Of course, this was incredibly sad for everyone. However, he did not let the sadness paralyze him and keep him from doing what what he could for the future. Indeed, just the opposite. Acknowledging his terminal condition gave him a new mission, a new assignment: there were new tasks to be completed, new perspectives to be considered, new conversations to be had, new decisions to be made, and new plans to be put in place.

If you are *aware* that you are in the final season of life, then you may consider yourself blessed indeed. It may sound strange, but this can be a gift, for such knowledge may bring a new clarity—the stakes are clear, and the ending point is understood. Like all who came before you and all who will come after you, you will die, and this is no longer a theoretical concept to you. You are actually on the way home, so it is time to plan for "a good walk home." You have been granted a season in which, by God's grace and the loving assistance of others, you can craft a fruitful and peaceful conclusion to your life's journey. To that end, I wrote this book for you.

When friends walk home together, they converse, and that's the way I would like to proceed here. I'm sure you have questions, and I have tried to anticipate what some of them might be. My focus will be on some of the more personal questions that come up in this time of life: questions about meaning, perspective, and spirituality. I'd like to concentrate on what you're thinking and how you are feeling, what your fears might be and what you envision for this final season of your life.

Others will accompany you on this journey, and you will want to talk with them as well: doctors, nurses, caregivers, social workers, a minister or spiritual counselor, an attorney, funeral home directors, family members, and friends. I won't be able to answer all your questions, and I'm not going to try. but I hope that I can point you in the right direction for some of those needs.

Right now, it's time for us to talk. Shall we walk together?

## CHAPTER ONE

# Time to come home!

*Living had got to be such a habit with him that
he couldn't conceive of any other condition.*

**FLANNERY O'CONNOR,
"A LATE ENCOUNTER WITH THE ENEMY"**

I REMEMBER WHEN MY PARENTS BOUGHT ME MY FIRST WATCH. Their motives were not pure. But then again, I had a tardiness problem. I was five or six years old at the time, an active little tyke who had too much fun playing with my friends late into the afternoon, so much fun in fact that I always found a way to ignore my mother's voice calling me home for supper. It must have made her absolutely crazy. In my imagination, I see mom and dad sitting down to talk about it.

"What are we going to do about Mike? He just won't listen to me when I call him to come home. I'm always worried that something has happened to him, even though I know he's just playing with his friends. But it's so frustrating! Supper gets cold and we all get angry. What are we going to do?"

"Why don't we buy him a watch?"

That worked for, like, a day.

You see, I learned quickly that watches (at least back then) needed to be set and wound to keep accurate time. I hatched an evil plot to overcome my dilemma, and the solution was simple: turn the time back, go home late as usual, and say, with my most convincing, exasperated voice, "I don't know what happened, Mom! I think my watch must have stopped! Look, it says it's 5:00, not 5:30."

Yeah, like they bought that.

This silly story from my childhood illustrates a point: there are many times in life when it may be time to go home, but we don't want to stop what we're doing to make the homeward trek. We're having too much fun. Like General Sash in Flannery O'Connor's short story "A Late Encounter with the Enemy," life has become such a habit, we can't conceive of it ending.

If you are reading this book, it probably means that you or someone you love has heard the call to come home. Playtime is over, the sun is low in the sky, you can smell supper cooking in kitchens throughout the neighborhood, and moms and dads are calling their children home. Let me say it more directly: you have reached an advanced age and know your time is short, or you have just seen a doctor look you in the eyes and say, "It's terminal. Nothing we can do will cure your illness. You have a limited time left before you die." It's time to go home.

If you're like me, that's a message you'd like to ignore or pretend you didn't hear. In your mind you are saying, "Just a little longer, just one more inning, just a few more baskets. I'll wait until my friends get called home too, and then we'll all leave together. We can't stop now—we're right in the middle of the best part of the game!" Nevertheless, you can't get the voice out of your head: "Time to come home!"

I currently serve as a hospice chaplain, and before that I was a pastor in several churches. Over the years I have visited many people who heard that call in various ways. Here are some of the ways the news came to them.

"Joe, you are getting close to ninety years old, and you have many health problems. Your time is limited, and I suggest you enjoy every day as much as you can."

"Folks, I'm sorry to tell you but your little boy has leukemia."

"It's a type of brain tumor called a glioblastoma, and it's inoperable."

"I'm afraid there's no heartbeat. Your little girl will be stillborn."

"Yes, I know he's in the prime of his life, but he has a

very aggressive form of pancreatic cancer. He may only have a few months at the most."

"Yes, an operation might help, but her heart is not strong enough for her to endure the surgery. All we can do is use medicine to manage her symptoms. I'm afraid she's failing."

"Yes, we could hit her cancer hard with chemotherapy and radiation, but in my opinion the best we could hope for is to extend her life a few more months, and the side effects will be severe. What would you like to do?"

People are getting news like this all the time—at this very moment in fact—learning that their time is at hand, the day is closing, and they are beginning the last leg of their earthly journey. Not one of us will avoid it. A minister I knew once used to say, "The statistics on death are staggering. One out of every one of us will die." No matter who we are, no matter how much fun we're having, no matter how much we've taken to the habit of living, at some point we will hear the call, "Time to come home!"

I was feeling sick one day, so I went to my doctor's office for what turned out to be an upper respiratory infection. My regular family practitioner was booked up, so the office staff set me up with one of her partners. I was delighted to find this other doctor was a kind, gentle man with a positive spirit, his gracious manner enhanced by a comforting, lilting Irish accent.

He checked me over and made his diagnosis. Then he wrote me a prescription, counseled me to rest, and gave a few other instructions. Then, as we were talking he discovered that I worked for hospice.

"Well," the physician responded, "my wife happens to be a hospice patient. She has end-stage ovarian cancer."

He paused, and almost immediately I realized I knew his wife. She wasn't one of our hospice patients, but I had met her before in our community and worked with her on a couple of projects. She was a lovely Irish Catholic lady who had devoted her life to visiting the sick and caring for the unfortunate. Margaret was one of those rare people who breathed encouragement, comfort, and affirmation into every situation she entered. I had had no idea about her condition.

The physician's halting words made it obvious that he needed to talk. So I found myself extending my stay in the examination room quite a bit past the usual exam and wrap-up. After the doctor described how his wife was doing, I asked about *him*. "I'm sorry, I didn't realize Margaret was so sick," I said. "How are you doing, Doc? Are you getting the support you need to cope with all this?"

"Well," he said, "she's handling it a lot better than I am. She seems to have accepted things. As for me, well, I've told her that's all well and good, but it doesn't mean I'm not going to be pissed off."

He chuckled at the same time a tear slipped down his reddened cheek. That was a surprisingly revealing, personal moment for a physician to have in front of a patient. I was honored that he felt comfortable enough to share it with me.

We talked a little more, and as I got ready to leave I asked him to give his dear wife a greeting, wishing both of them help and encouragement from God. In reply, the physician indicated that it had been good to talk. Little had I expected that a trip to the doctor for my needs would turn into an opportunity to minister to the doctor for *his* needs.

We never know, do we? Every day and in every place, in every season of life and in a variety of circumstances, people hear the message that it's time to come home.

Sometimes, this seems natural. When I visit elderly hospice patients, folks in their eighties or nineties, there can be a sense, even in the sadness, that death is expected. The person has lived a full, long life, and everyone knows that the finish line is somewhere in the vicinity. Such a death brings its own forms of grief, but the shock of untimeliness is not part of the equation.

I find the atmosphere quite different when someone in the prime of life becomes terminally ill.

We had a patient in his thirties who died quickly from a particularly aggressive form of cancer. Earlier that year, his wife had lost a baby. Then, in the fall, she discovered she was pregnant again. While they were grieving their loss and rejoicing in another opportunity to welcome life into their family, he got sick. The diagnosis was pronounced, and before you knew it, he and his wife were taking walks through the halls of the cancer center, sitting through chemo appointments, and finding their life turned upside down once more.

She had her baby. Shortly after that, she lost her husband. Now she is a widow with a toddler and a newborn, and a bereaved mother who lost a baby. In less than a year, everything had changed.

Frankly, I'm not sure how anybody could be ready for something like that. But it happens, and it behooves us all to be realistic about life's uncertainty.

Of course, no one can live in constant fear and dread, but we can all be aware that bad things happen, sometimes to the most unlikely people, and we can try to build the kinds of supports into our lives that will bear us up when sudden storms threaten to overwhelm us.

As he aged, Henri Nouwen, the priest and teacher, thought more and more about the final season of life and its ending, and how he as a person of faith might learn to "befriend his death." In his book *Our Greatest Gift: A Meditation on Dying and Caring,* he reflected,

> While sitting alone in my little hermitage, I realize how unprepared I am to die....
>
> ...Am I willing to make that journey? Am I willing to let go of whatever power I have left, to unclench my fists and trust in the grace hidden in complete powerlessness? I don't know. I really don't know. It seems impossible, since everything alive in me protests against this journey into nothingness.

Yes, "everything alive in [us] protests against this." Here we are, right in the middle of the best part of the game, and mom's calling me to come home?

Makes you wish you could turn your watch back, doesn't it?

## CHAPTER TWO

# How can I accept the fact that I'm going to die and yet not "give up"?

*As our time winds down, we all seek comfort in simple
pleasures—companionship, everyday routines, the taste
of good food, the warmth of sunlight on our faces.
We become less interested in the rewards of achieving
and accumulating, and more interested in the rewards
of simply being. Yet while we may feel less ambitious,
we also become concerned for our legacy. And we have
a deep need to identify purposes outside ourselves
that make living feel meaningful and worthwhile.*

❧ **ATUL GAWANDE**, BEING MORTAL

BESS WAS "REALLY SOMETHING."

I heard that a number of times over the course of my visit. Her family loved her but fully acknowledged that she was her own woman, independent to a fault. She knew what she wanted and usually got it without a lot of fuss or bother. Try arguing with her, and you would find out quickly: Bess was "really something."

Once, after a stint in a rehab facility where they had a small aviary with birds, she liked it so much that she came home and had one built for herself, with a glass front so she could watch them climbing the branches, feeding, and fluttering around. She placed it in her living room, filled it with birds, and spent the rest of her days enjoying them. She set cages in other rooms too, surrounding herself with little winged creatures who would otherwise be off somewhere, flying freely in the sky were it not for Bess exerting her loving will over them. The house echoed with their chirping as Bess ruled over her feathery paradise.

Well into her nineties, Bess had outlived her friends. She'd proudly let you know that she was the oldest living member of her church, an old mainline Protestant congregation downtown with one of the most beautiful sanctuaries in the city. Her mom was Baptist and her father Catholic, but her grandfather attended this particular church. When she got old enough, Bess's parents let her choose which church she wanted to attend, and one Sunday morning she went with grandpa to try his out. One look at the glorious altar, appointments, and stained glass, and she knew immediately that this was where she wanted to be. The atmosphere was suitably regal for a young princess like her. She remained a member all her life.

When Bess came into hospice care, she still lived in her home, functioned independently, and asked for help only when she needed it. She wasn't even sure she required our care team that much. Most patients see the nurse once or twice a week, but Bess wouldn't hear of it. Once every two weeks it would be. The social worker and chaplain were lucky if we received permission to come monthly. Not that she wasn't hospitable; she just had her terms. Our visits were always pleasant. She wasn't snobby or standoffish; I think she truly liked people and enjoyed visitors and conversation—when she wanted them.

Bess didn't allow her daughter to come and stay with her until the final two weeks of her life. By then, Bess was having trouble breathing and found herself getting weaker. She feared falling. So she called her daughter and told her it was time.

She wasn't ready for the bed yet, though. In her mind, that came later. Bess had a long sofa in the TV room where she and her daughter spent most of their time, near her favorite parrot. They both slept on that sofa each night. When the nurse suggested she get a hospital bed, just in case, Bess wouldn't hear of it. First of all, it wasn't practical. Her tiny cluttered house couldn't absorb one, and she had no desire to change anything around anyway. No, when it was time, her own bed would work just fine. You got the idea that Bess would let you know when that time came.

The last time I visited Bess was a few days before she died, and we sat on the sofa and talked. Then, over the weekend she moved to her bed (by her decision), and it looked like she wasn't getting out again. I called on Monday to schedule a visit. Bess's daughter, unlike her mother, did not hesitate for a moment in asking me to come. When I arrived, Bess was in bed under the covers, oxygen tubing draped over her face, looking drawn and tired. She smiled and talked to me in response to my greeting, but it was hard to understand her. I said a prayer asking God to bless her with comfort and peace and to help her family. I encouraged her to rest, and she smiled again and closed her eyes.

A few days later, early in the morning, the office called and notified me that Bess had died. I met the nurse at the home. Bess lay in her bed, her daughter and grandchildren sitting beside her. We prayed together, then the nurse and I took care of details, made phone calls, and ensured the family had what they needed. After a while, shortly before the team from the funeral home arrived, we went to the bedroom one last time to see how everyone was doing.

They were talking about Bess, about how she was "really something." Someone commented on the beautiful satin dressing gown she was wearing.

Her daughter perked up. "You know, it was the strangest thing. Just last evening, I bathed mom and was getting ready to put clean pajamas on her. But she said no, she didn't want them. Then, as she laid there naked, she told me to go to the closet in the spare room and get a green box off the shelf. I retrieved it and inside was this lovely gown, brand new. Mom had me put it on her and then cover her up again. Then she looked at me and said, 'Okay, it's time. Let's get on with it.' Now, this morning, she's gone."

That Bess, she was really something. If ever I met someone who was in control of her life until the end, it was she. Many of us don't get that privilege and must cede some, if not most, control to others. However, that doesn't mean we have to "give up." There is a difference between accepting that I am in the final season of my life and "giving up."

I have to clarify this with hospice patients and their families all the time. When someone opts for hospice or "comfort" care, peohple all too often equate that with throwing in the towel. When a patient accepts a prognosis of impending death, it may seem to family members that their loved one has abandoned hope and lost the will to keep fighting. Sometimes the patient herself might think that way. However, that need not be the case. Extending the length of one's life is not the only thing for which to fight.

When it's time to switch from "curative" care to "comfort" care, a difficult transition in thinking becomes necessary. A terminal diagnosis has been given and accepted. What does that mean? It means, first, that those involved have made a realistic assessment: a cure is no longer possible. Second, it indicates that the goals for the patient's care must therefore change. Note: there are still goals. No one is giving up. There are significant steps that can still be taken for the patient's benefit. Important things remain for which to fight. No one is raising a white flag and surrendering at this point, but we are shifting the focus of the battle.

But this does require a different way of thinking. Throughout most of our lives, we avail ourselves of ordinary medical care. We get sick, and medical care helps us get better. If we get a serious illness or injury that threatens our life, it "fixes" us so that we heal and our life is extended. But what happens when "getting better" is no longer feasible? What do we do when there is no "fix"? What if any significant extension of our life is not in the cards? What if there is a slight chance of extending the duration of our life, but it may involve sacrificing much *quality* of life? This is the moment in which people have to consider more than the ordinary medical questions we are used to asking.

Ordinary medical care and treatment alone can't help us fulfill all of our most important goals, especially at the end of life. It becomes the task of those who have received a terminal diagnosis (along with their loved ones and advocates) to define what they want during the last season of their life and to get good counsel that will pay attention not only to their medical needs but also their personal, emotional, relational, and spiritual needs, desires, dreams, and wishes.

In *Being Mortal*, Dr. Atul Gawande says most people want to make their own decisions about how to proceed with their end-of-life care, but they would like to do so with good information and guidance from providers who care for their patients and respect their unique goals. They don't want "paternalistic" doctors who act as medical authorities and insist that they alone know what is best for the patient. Nor do they want "informative" doctors who merely give them information and leave the choices entirely up to the patient. Instead, they want "interpretive" doctors who will help patients and families determine what is most important to them and how they can achieve that.

When working with his patients, Dr. Gawande asks three questions to help them sort out their priorities and make wise decisions:

- What are your biggest fears and concerns?

- What goals are most important to you?

- What trade-offs are you willing to make,
  and what ones are you not?

Answering questions like these honestly can empower us to make good care choices as we face the final stretch of life. That is not giving up; that is exercising the God-given capacity for reasoning, communicating, and decision-making. We are not choosing death—that is already in the picture and beyond our control. We are choosing how we would like to live the final portion of our life. We are choosing dignity. We want to have a good walk home.

For example, your greatest fear might be that you will have to be in a hospital or extended care facility when you would rather be at home with your loved ones in familiar and comfortable surroundings. You are afraid of the pain and symptoms associated with your disease. You don't want to be miserable, but you also want to stay coherent and conversant as long as possible so that you can spend quality time with the important people in your life. But you don't want to have to go to doctor's appointments three times a week either. You would like to stay active and ambulatory as long as possible, and when walking is no longer safe or possible, you'd still like to sit outside in your yard sometimes or occasionally have dinner out or attend a church service. Perhaps there is one more trip you'd like to make to a place that is special to you.

Being able to voice these kinds of wishes and having the freedom to choose them is the exact opposite of giving up. Enlisting the care and support you will require to achieve such goals will involve effort, choices, and adaptations. You may have to fight to get what you need. Let no one think that this is about abandoning hope or lying down to die. Choosing comfort care or hospice care is not about giving up and surrendering to death. Yes, a terminal diagnosis has been given. Yes, we know what the ultimate outcome will be. But there is a season of life that is still to be lived until that day. You are alive, a person of dignity with wishes, hopes, and dreams. There are resources to access; there are priorities to pursue. Acceptance does not equal "giving up."

Life is made up of different seasons through which we pass, each with its own possibilities, challenges, and tasks. On the day we are born, we emerge into a new season of life: from the womb, we enter infancy. During that season, we bond with our family and begin to develop as separate human beings. Then we become toddlers, then school-age children, then teenagers, then young adults. Changes force us to make necessary adjustments along the way, and it is hoped that we make them in positive, healthy ways. Adulthood likewise finds us taking different paths and moving through various stages. Each life door through which we pass presents us with changes that require us to pay attention and adapt.

Each season of life has its dreams, goals, and tasks. The final season of life is no different.

So, as we walk together, let me ask you:

- What does it mean for you to have a good quality of life in this season of walking home?

- As you age or as your disease progresses, what is most important to you? What dreams and goals do you have about how you would like to live out the final chapter of your life?

- What are your fears and concerns?

- What unfinished business is there that you would like to complete before you leave this world for the next?

- What gifts would you like to leave your loved ones as you prepare to depart? What would you like them to remember most about you?

These are personal questions, with unique answers for each person and family. I would not presume to know what the answers might be for you, other than to say that this is the time in life when virtues like faith, hope, and love are meant to come to fruition. Whatever specific choices you make, I'm sure you will want your experience to be filled with qualities like these so that you can write the final chapters in your life story with a satisfying conclusion.

> All we ask is to be allowed to remain the writers
> of our own story ❦ **ATUL GAWANDE**, *Being Mortal*

I can't think of a better example of someone who "wrote her own story" than Lottie.

Lottie and I met eight years ago when she became a hospice patient. I went for my initial visit and we sat in the living room and talked. Her husband, who was suspicious of "preachers" of any kind, wasn't sure he wanted me to come. Every time he'd ever gone to church, he growled, all they wanted was to empty his wallet! Throughout the visit, he sat in a chair behind me and I had to turn my head uncomfortably to include him in the conversation. It was clear he was trying to make me fidget.

Lottie was a tough woman from the hills of Kentucky. Her husband was an even tougher man from Tennessee. He ran away from home at age fifteen, came all the way up to Indianapolis, and went right to work. He married young, divorced soon after, and had a son in tow when he met Lottie, herself a young woman far from home in the big city. They fell in love, married, had another son, and lived the life of blue-collar working people in the rust belt.

Now, many years later, Lottie had been diagnosed with a terminal lung disease. I asked her what her goal was for this season of life when I met her on that July day eight years ago.

"I want to plant flowers in my garden in the spring," she said.

Knowing full well that this might not happen, I commended her for her positive, forward-looking spirit, and I told her I would be there to enjoy them with her.

Lottie did indeed plant her flowers that next spring and enjoyed them fully, and I was there to share the joy with her. And she did it again the next year. And the next year. In fact, for *seven* springs, the gardens in front of Lottie's house bloomed. Our hospice team kept visiting and marveling at her spirit.

Over the course of that time, her husband was diagnosed with cancer, came on to the hospice service, and died. (By the way, we had become fast friends by that time. He stopped sitting behind me and we enjoyed many face-to-face conversations. He even asked me to officiate his funeral service. I guess I was the one preacher who never asked him for money over the years, and he came to appreciate me listening to his stories and praying for him when I visited.)

Lottie also had a little dog that she and her family adored. The poor little thing became quite ill during the course of Lottie's hospice care, with tumors protruding from her underside, making it hard for her to walk or lie down comfortably. The dog died one day, but Lottie lived on, now bereft of all but her grandson, who cared for her daily, and her son and granddaughter, who lived nearby.

They set up a bed in Lottie's living room, and then eventually she moved into what had been the dining room so that she could have easier access to the bathroom and more privacy. The hospice team continued to visit, and we continued to be astounded that this woman just kept going. Even though she spent most of each day in bed and slept much of the time, she never did become bed bound. To the end, she was able to get up and walk to the bathroom, though her oxygen stats would plummet whenever she did.

Lottie remained coherent and hospitable to the end. She engaged every member of our team in conversation on our visits until the day she died. She always welcomed me praying for her. She kept smiling, kept persevering, kept writing her remarkable story of a final season of life that lasted years beyond the day when she received a terminal diagnosis.

Lottie and her family had become so much a part of our lives that we could scarcely believe it when we heard she had died. I officiated her funeral with tears.

A week later I wrote the following poem to honor her simple faith and steadfast spirit.

When first we met in summer
it seemed as though that fall would be her last,
one final Christmas if by strength.

But she from tough Kentucky stock
and hills that had withstood the mines
        and stills and feuds,
determined, spoke of other plans:

I'll plant my flowers in spring,
outlast the winter and get out on my porch to sit
and see them bloom again.

I smiled and said I'd pray;
it couldn't hurt to ask for such a simple thing.
And so I did

though folks like her quite seldom
get what they ask, for death sits at their shoulders
soon to drag them off.

Death did not know her well enough!
He took her husband, dog, and others too
but every spring she smiled.

For seven springs in fact
the flowers bloomed in beds and pots around her porch
and she, determined, carried on

While I kept praying year by year,
shaking my head to see that life could be so strong
and she so constant.

When death took her this winter
I'd like to think she finally just gave him permission,
determined to the end.

Perhaps she'd had a dream:
some Gardener calling out for help in spring
to tend his beds

and bring new color to his porch,

where he finds pleasure visiting with those

whose help comes from the hills.

Every time I left Lottie's house after a visit, walking through the front door I would hear her call out, "Now you be careful going down those steps, Mike."

As I grasped the handrail and descended them, I'd glance over at the front porch, with its big pots filled with flowers, and at the gardens in the yard, shake my head, and smile.

There comes a day when each human being, if life is not taken in an untimely manner, will be forced to accept that he or she is approaching the end of life. But we need not feel like this is "giving up." There is still life to be lived at the end of life. Our story is not yet fully told.

As the Apostle Paul testified: "The time of my departure is at hand. I have competed well; I have finished the race; I have kept the faith" (2 Timothy 4:6–7). Each of us likewise has a competition to complete, a race to run, a faith journey to fulfill. If you have been given the privilege of knowing you have reached one of the last laps, you and your loved ones can look ahead to the finish line and decide, with God's wisdom, how you want to get there.

Thankfully, no one is left alone to face these challenges. When the aged patriarch Jacob looked back on his life, he spoke of "the God who has been my shepherd from my birth to this day...." (Genesis 48:15). The same God who brought us into the world will shepherd us out of it as well, all the way to the end and safely home, providing goodness and lovingkindness every day of our lives so that we might choose wisely and complete our journey well.

God doesn't want any of us to give up. He wants to lead us on a good walk home.

**CHAPTER THREE**

# How can I experience God's presence in my final season of life?

*By the sacred anointing of the sick and the prayer of the priests the whole Church commends those who are ill to the suffering and glorified Lord, that he may raise them up and save them. **And indeed she exhorts them to contribute to the good of the People of God by freely uniting themselves to the Passion and death of Christ.***

✠ *CATECHISM OF THE CATHOLIC CHURCH, NO. 1499,*
(EMPHASIS ADDED)

IT WAS A BRIEF VISIT. THE STAFF NURSE IN THE HOSPITAL told me that our hospice patient in the room down the hall was not a religious man and did not care to see the chaplain. However, she said, his daughter asked for me to come see him. So I went.

The patient was minimally responsive; opening his eyes, he responded to my greeting with a nod and a mumbled hello and then laid his head back down on the pillow, showing no more interest. His daughter was concerned for his spiritual well-being. It wasn't that he was anti-religion or anything. He just hadn't seen much of a need for going to church or observing religious practices throughout his life. She wanted me to pray for him now as he neared the end of his life.

I asked the patient if he would like that, and he nodded and grunted his permission. I prayed for God's peace to fill him. I prayed for comfort of body and serenity in his spirit. I prayed that he would be at peace with God, with himself, and with others, and that his heart would not be troubled or afraid but that he would know the presence of God in his hour of need. I asked the same for his family.

After encouraging her to call with further support needs, I left and went to the nurses' station to do my documentation. It was my final visit of the day and I was ready to go home; so when the paperwork was complete, I took the elevator down and walked out of the hospital to my car. About fifteen minutes later I received a call while driving down the road. "Ms. Franklin here on the unit is with her father and she would like a chaplain visit."

"Are you sure?" I asked. "I was just there."

"Yes, she came down the nurses' station and specifically asked for the chaplain. She seemed animated and concerned."

"Okay, I'll be there in a few minutes."

So I went back, parked, and made my way directly to the room. The patient's eyes were closed, and he looked comfortable and peaceful. The daughter, however, jumped up when she saw me and began talking immediately.

"I have to tell you what happened after you prayed," she began breathlessly. "I went over to the bed to make sure my dad was comfortable before I left to get some supper. And he woke up, sat up wide awake, and was looking over my shoulder. 'There he is!' he said. I thought maybe he was talking about you or one of the aides, but there was no one else in the room, and he just kept saying, 'There he is!' and 'Can't you see him?'"

"'Who, dad?' I kept asking, and he finally said, 'It's Jesus!' Then he said, 'Call the chaplain!' So I had the nurses call you. Did he really see Jesus?"

Was I supposed to know how to answer that? To this day I can't.

When people ask about knowing the presence of God in the midst of their terminal illness or death, I sometimes think this is the kind of experience they imagine. Honestly, I have heard about plenty of them. From seeing Jesus himself to seeing angels, saints, deceased loved ones, little children, or other "heavenly representatives," patients and families have reported to our hospice team a variety of visions, experiences, and impressions. Sometimes the impressions were audible: voices, music, bells, a certain moving of the wind. On other occasions patients and families have witnessed curious events that they have interpreted as "signs." One patient loved birds, for example, and right before she died a bird perched outside her window and then flew away into the sky at the moment she passed.

These curious occurrences get our attention, seem to add a level of meaning to sad situations, and bring a measure of comfort. I have little doubt that God can grant such blessings, and I never discount that possibility when presented with someone's experience. However, it must also be said that I've never known anyone to have control over such things happening. If these experiences are from God, then it appears to be God's choice and God's alone as to when and where and for whom they take place.

Therefore, if someone asks me, "How can I know the presence of God in my final season of life?" I wouldn't counsel that person to expect the extraordinary vision, impression, or sign. Instead, I would encourage him to seek God's help through more ordinary means of grace—prayer, Scripture, spiritual reading, the sacraments of the church, other spiritual practices, and so on. (We'll talk more about spiritual practices in a later chapter.)

I do have one unequivocal piece of counsel. If a person genuinely wants to know the presence of God in the midst of his sufferings, I would urge that person to look for God primarily in the *love* of those around him.

> Beloved, if God so loved us, we also must love one another. No one has ever seen God. Yet, if we love one another, God remains in us, and his love is brought to perfection in us.  ❧ 1 JOHN 4:11–12

Daniel was only eighteen years old when he died. He was one of the brightest students in our local high school, a star athlete with much future potential, and one of the biggest personalities you'll ever meet.

One autumn evening, my wife and I sat with his parents at a football game in which our sons were playing. Daniel had to come out of the contest when he complained of a severe headache. We were concerned, but didn't consider this unusual. The boy played hard and seemed always to be in the middle of the action and collisions that are a part of varsity football.

However, the headaches continued for the better part of a month, and one day his parents took him to the emergency room. It soon became clear that Daniel's headaches and symptoms were not the result of a concussion or head injury. Test results revealed that he had a brain tumor.

I was there with dozens and dozens of other people from our community the night the brain surgeon came out and broke the news to the family about the results of the biopsy. His dad and I went for a walk, and I listened as he tried to express the shock and dismay he felt.

And thus began a journey that lasted about a year and a half until Daniel died in the early morning hours of Memorial Day, 2006.

I don't know how many times I visited the hospital over those months, but it seems like every time I did, Daniel and his family were surrounded by people from our community. They themselves are among the strongest, most resilient and steadfast people

I have ever known, but who can face something like this alone? So others stepped up in a big way.

Daniel's father wrote a book about his son and their experience, called *Small Victories: A Legacy of Courage and Love*. In it, he quoted a local newspaper article:

> After Daniel died, his father thanked the community for its support and offered some final thoughts: "In a community like [ours], it seems, at least for us, there was help around every corner. Frequently, we as parents forget that therein lies the value of living in a community like [ours]....We drew our strength in large part from [a caring community], and for that we can't possibly thank you enough."

I had the opportunity to speak at a public memorial service for Daniel. In my message, I noted how the death of a promising young person leads us to say things like, "This doesn't seem real," or, "I just can't fathom this." But then I testified to the fact that, in the midst of the unreality of the situation, many things had become even more real to me.

First, I remarked that I'd come to see even more clearly that suffering is real and terrible and heartbreaking. But second, I said, I had observed that love is real and that it is the most important thing to experience and practice in a world when suffering that seems "unreal" touches our lives.

So many of you have followed Jesus' example and laid down your lives in both small and great ways to show love and to bring help and comfort into this situation over the past year and a half.

As a result, many very real miracles took place. Laughter was heard in places where sorrow sought to overwhelm. Comfort and encouragement overcame despair. Renewed strength and energy overcame exhaustion. Hundreds of "small victories" were won. Individuals, families, and communities were strengthened. We all learned about integrity, discipline, determination, hopefulness and faith.

Love is real, and it's the most important thing in a world where suffering is real. By love we overcome.

◁ *From **Small Victories**, by* **JEFF MERCER**

Christian Wiman is one of our best poets and authors. In his book *My Bright Abyss: Meditation of a Modern Believer,* he describes his thoughts, feelings, and religious doubts, questions, and yearnings during seven years of battling a rare form of cancer. It is an excruciatingly honest meditation on both the absence and presence of God in our suffering. Wiman has much to say about faith and doctrine, and church and religious practice, as well as the role of art and poetry in finding meaning in life, but in the end, he says, he found God's presence most fully displayed in the love of other people.

Wiman says, out of his own experience, that in suffering, even

the most devout do not long for some kind of meditative commu-
nion with God, some mystical divine connection. What we really
want is to know that God loves us. And we know that best when
we are surrounded by human love. "What one craves is supernat-
ural love, but one finds it only within human love," he writes.

Before his death, Jesus summarized what he had taught his disciples: "I have told you this so that you might have peace in me. In
the world you will have trouble, but take courage, I have con-
quered the world" (John 16:33). How did Jesus overcome this
evil world with all its troubles? By loving the people of the world
and laying down his life for them. He overcame suffering and
death by acts of sacrificial love.

Even so, we overcome through love.

If love is God's answer to human suffering, then knowing God
in our sufferings will involve immersing ourselves ever more deeply into loving relationships. "No one has ever seen God. Yet, if we
love one another, God remains in us, and his love is brought to
perfection in us."

Some of us tend to withdraw from others when we need loving
interaction most. There is some natural withdrawal that takes
place in the end of life, but I am speaking of a different kind here,
the kind by which we envelop ourselves within ourselves, too
proud, self-absorbed, or afraid to open our hearts to others, when
we close ourselves off to love by choice or habit.

Opening ourselves up to receiving and giving love is one way
to follow the teaching of the church when it exhorts the suffering
to "contribute to the good of the People of God by freely uniting

themselves to the Passion and death of Christ." It is preeminently through Jesus that we know what love is. How Jesus acted and spoke during his dying as he related to his friends and others around him sets forth an ultimate example of divine and human love. The affection that flows between us as we receive care and support from our families and friends in our seasons of need is a reflection of his self-giving love.

- On the night of his betrayal, he humbled himself and washed his disciples' feet—*in love.*

- He hosted a meal and served his disciples, giving them his Body and Blood to nourish them—*in love.*

- He spoke words of comfort to them, explaining why he had to go away, and promising that they would never be abandoned—*in love.*

- He listened patiently to their questions and concerns and gave them his gift of peace—*in love.*

- He prayed for them and asked the Father to protect them and keep them as one—*in love.*

- He accepted the Father's will, to take the cup of suffering for them—*in love.*

- He subjected himself to arrest, trial, scourging and humiliation, death on a cross, and burial in the tomb—*in love.*

- From the cross he spoke words for us to hear, from which to draw strength: words of forgiveness, hope, caring, lament, suffering, fulfillment, and trust—*in love.*

"He loved his own in the world and he loved them to the end" (John 13:1). Jesus loved those around him with genuine love. Love means being with another and giving oneself for the other's benefit, and this is what Jesus did. He sacrificed for his friends. He listened and spoke with them. He served them. He saved them through his loving presence, words, and actions.

The man's tears were unsettling. There is something about a man crying uncontrollably that shakes me. His dying wife was in the bed across the room, speaking occasionally, but mostly lying with eyes closed, comfortable but waning. He cried for her. He cried for himself. He cried for the fact that he was losing the life they had shared for decades.

In particular, he was anxious about finances. Long the family provider, he now saw bills filling the mailbox day after day, from the usual utilities to the extraordinary medical bills, and he knew the funds in his bank account were insufficient to cover them. The one area he had always controlled was now beyond his control. As for other matters, he knew he was in over his head. He had to trust the doctors and medical experts with regard to his wife's condition. He didn't worry much about his kids anymore. They had grown and were taking care of their own lives now. But the money—he had been careful about that. These should have been their golden years, when the money he had earned and they had saved together would support them in a life of modest comfort.

Instead, he found himself with a futile finger in the dike, water leaking and spraying around it into his face, the wall bulging and threatening to overwhelm him with a torrent of flood waters any moment.

I didn't know what to say to him. Thankfully, I'm part of a team, and we have wonderful social workers who are creative and knowledgeable about sources of help in time of need. I made a note to call the team. As for me, I listened to this sad man, prayed with him and his wife, put my hand on his shoulder, and tried to encourage him as we sat together, the oxygen concentrator humming away in the little bedroom of their humble house.

Then he told me a story that grabbed hold of my heart and I couldn't stop thinking about it for days afterward. It both saddened and inspired me. As I meditated upon it, I realized that this man was not only upset about his money situation. He was losing his life. A way of living and relating to others in his community was passing away. However, there was still a heartbeat, still a bit of breath, still enough life and love in the old neighborhood to give a person hope.

My friend and his wife were in the habit of patronizing a little corner store and cafe down the street. Over the years, they rarely missed a day sharing a cup of coffee or a bowl of soup for lunch. That's where they read the paper, saw their neighbors, caught up on the latest news and gossip. This is where the people in their world bragged about their kids' exploits, argued about local polix tics and community issues, complained about the weather, and played the roles they had adopted among their friends.

They loved that little restaurant and gathering place. It was as much a part of their life together as their own living room. However, when my friend's wife got sick, it became more and more difficult to go. Finally, they had to stop altogether. The man felt bad about this. He felt so bad that one day he called and talked to the owner, told him he was sorry they hadn't been by for awhile, and expressed his regret that the store had to lose their business. He apologized—as if it weren't right that the business should suffer just because his wife got sick.

If my mouth didn't drop when I heard that, I don't know why. Who does a thing like that these days? Who goes out of his way to make a phone call and say "I'm sorry" to the owner of a business when he and his family can't afford to support it any longer? Come to think of it, who still thinks of shopping or eating out as "supporting a business" and its workers? Who considers merchants personal friends? Who sees life in the community as so intertwined and organically connected that one thinks he needs to apologize when he can't do his part as a customer because of difficult circumstances? This was remarkable love.

Then he told me more. He shared how the other day he'd heard a knock on the door. Leaving his wife's side, he answered it and was greeted by a woman who worked at that corner store. In her arms she carried a big paper bag filled with food. Along with it, she handed him an envelope that contained a get-well card and a couple of twenty-dollar bills. A small token of love. Probably all that a struggling inner-city shop owner could afford to send to help a neighbor in need.

The message? Apology accepted, or rather, apology not necessary. We understand. We're in this together. Thank you for being part of our lives. You still are, whether you can buy our stuff or not. You live down the street. We try to take care of each other around here.

As I left his home, I climbed behind the wheel of my car and pulled out, turning off the radio and driving in silence. In an old neighborhood where few travel, where the sidewalks are crumbling and the streets are uneven, where on some streets grass grows unmown around boarded-up houses, where people have lived and worked and raised families since World War II and some have never left, an old woman lay dying, a man wept, and I caught a glimpse of Jesus in a simple story of grace—neighborliness and love.

It took my breath away.

How will you know the presence of God in your final season of life? By immersing yourself in this kind of love—God's love!—as it is reflected in the presence, words, and actions you share with those around you, through giving and receiving such love, and by holding it in your heart.

Such love is not some lofty ideal, concept, or disembodied virtue. It is as down to earth as the basin, water, and towel by which Jesus knelt down on his knees, took dirty feet in his hands, and cleansed them. You will feel it through a family member's touch. You will hear it in words of reassurance from a friend. You will see it in the tireless and often thankless work of a caregiver. You may see it in the delivery of a paper bag full of food and a bit of cash help. Others will see it in you as you practice kindness, forbearance, and faithfulness toward them.

This is practical, hands-on, face-to-face, heart-to-heart *human* love. At times, for patients and caregivers alike, it may be uncomfortable to realize how up close and personal this love will have to be. Bodies will need to be washed and clothed, wounds tended and dressed. Soiled clothes and sheets will have to be changed. Tears will be shed. Doubts, fears, discouragements, and frustrations will be expressed. A person may find he needs a little financial help. There will be emergencies in the middle of the night; folks will lose sleep and get tired and grumpy. Angry words will be exchanged, feelings hurt. There will be need for much patience, forbearance, confession, and forgiveness. This is as down-to-earth as it gets.

The potential for such raw intimacy can make us feel vulnerable, hesitant, and anxious. But is this not the very context in which love "bears all things, believes all things, hopes all things, endures all things" (1 Corinthians 13:7)?

You ask how you can know God's presence in this final season of your life. Perhaps God will come to you in some extraordinary way, through an ecstatic or otherworldly kind of vision or experience. I can't say. But who's to say the kind of practical, inelegant, "ordinary" love I've described above isn't pretty extraordinary in its own way?

The way I see it, this is the kind of love Jesus showed us, and sharing it with each other might turn out to be a pretty good way of experiencing his loving presence with us today.

## CHAPTER FOUR

# How can I make my death a gift to others?

*How can I now live so that my death will be an optimal blessing for my family, my church, and the world?*

❧ **RONALD ROLHEISER,** SACRED FIRE

MY GRANDMOTHER ANNABELLE WAS A GIVER, AND I HAVE BEEN and continue to be a grateful recipient of her many gifts.

Annabelle was raised by my great-grandmother Grace, whose husband died in his thirties after a farming accident. She raised five children and lived until age 103. Her daughter Annabelle didn't fall far from the tree. She also lost her husband at a young age, and like her mother before her, she made the choice to embrace the challenge of overcoming her loss.

She lived in Chicago and had never driven an automobile, for example. But after my grandpa died she got her license so that she could be self-sufficient, involved in her church, and able to visit her friends. She blossomed into an active, generous woman who followed her Lord and served her neighbors. This is the Annabelle I remember most: one who served others. She had a group of elderly women she saw regularly, assisting them with their needs, transporting them around the city, being their friend and helper.

Annabelle cared deeply about her family too, but we had all moved away from Chicago, so we communicated primarily through phone calls and letters. I know for a fact she prayed for us on a regular basis too. I saw her once during college when she had her pastor invite us for a concert, and our gospel team sang in her church. After I graduated, she traveled east to attend my wedding and present my bride and me with a generous check so that we could have a nice honeymoon. We moved to Vermont and once hosted her and my other grandmother during fall foliage season, and I think she was pleased that I had entered the ministry. I still have the books about Jesus she gave me when I was baptized as an infant, books she hoped I'd read as I grew up. The seeds of her loving generosity in my life were planted early.

I returned to Chicago to attend seminary several years later, and this gave us a chance to see each other more often. Her generous financial support toward my schooling was a great blessing, and she also helped us furnish our modest home. We used to take Annabelle around the lake to Michigan to see her mother on her birthday each year as she approached, reached, and surpassed age 100.

A few years after seminary our family moved to Indiana, and

Annabelle relocated to Maryland, to a continuing care community near my parents. She meant this as a gift. She didn't want to be a burden to her children or grandchildren, so she set herself up in a place where she could live and be cared for, and no one would ever have to worry about getting a call one day to fly to Chicago and take care of things. So Annabelle left her home and made a new one late in life where she could have her own life and activities but be close to some of her family as well.

Through the years, my grandma Annabelle continued to bless me with gifts. When my church began taking mission trips to India, she was one of our biggest contributors. In fact, it was while I was on one of those trips, half a world away, that Annabelle died. This was a shock because my grandmother was such a strong woman—and after all, her mother had lived to be 103! Nevertheless, the heart of this kind woman who spent her life giving to others simply stopped beating one day, and we were all the poorer for it.

The morning after I heard of my grandmother's passing, I needed some time alone, so I got up early and walked around the large courtyard next to our hotel, where workmen were constructing a lavish stage for a Hindu wedding. It was one of the few times in my adult life that I have openly wept. But I took comfort in the fact that I was right where she wanted me to be, doing something that she had given generously to support.

Nor has Annabelle's giving to me ceased. It has been over ten years now since I left parish ministry as a pastor, and it was a hard leaving. I wasn't sure what I would do, but soon an opportunity came for me to take a chaplain position with a local hospice. Over time I have come to see this as a perfect vocation for me, and I think I know where that comes from. I have reflected on my grandmother's example often while doing this work. As she found her greatest joy in visiting and befriending her elderly friends, so now I get the chance to do similar work each day all around the city where I live. Annabelle's spirit lives on, and I feel that in some way she imparted a portion of it to me. I pray that I will be as faithful and giving as she was.

In her life and in her death, my grandmother gave me gifts. Spiritual teachers such as Henri Nouwen and Ronald Rolheiser (*Sacred Fire*, p. 284f) suggest that one of the great questions in the final season of life is: "How can I live now so that my final days and death will be a gift to my family and those around me?" Rolheiser calls this "giving our death away." A time will come when we are no longer as active in life, working hard and expending energy to make the world a better place. Is there still a contribution we can make? As we enter the final season of life, can we even make our diminishing and dying a blessing to others?

This question brings us back to the *Catechism* and its call to link our death with Jesus' Passion and death. From the moment he was baptized, our Lord had an active and effective ministry, and as that work concluded, Jesus was able to say to his Father, "I glorified you on earth by accomplishing the work that you gave me to do" (John 17:4). As we all know, however, Jesus had more to contribute after he said those words in the Upper Room.

Jesus went on to give us the gift of his death. In contrast to his *active* ministry of teaching, healing, and training disciples, the death he died was an act of loving *passivity*—he laid down his life for us. Jesus was betrayed, tried, scourged, humiliated, led to Golgotha, crucified, taken down from the cross, and laid in a tomb. Note those passive verbs. In the end, he sacrificed control of his own destiny and allowed others to seal his fate. Jesus submitted himself to death for our sake, and as a result the world was blessed with redemption and new life.

In the final season of our lives, we must learn the value of a more passive contribution as well. Our ability to do active work in the world diminishes as we come to the end of our shift, and then we have a new, more passive, contribution to make. We pass on a measure of responsibility and control to others. At the same time, we hope that we can play a different role that will still be life-giving and nourishing to those around us.

When John the Baptizer saw that his active role was ending and that it was time for him to give the more active place to Jesus, he said, "He must increase; I must decrease" (John 3:30). In the final season of life, we too must make this kind of transition. We die to life as we have known it so that our death may become a gift to others.

How this proceeds specifically will vary with each individual. Often, because of infirmity and illness, our passive contribution to the world will play out in very earthy ways. We will have to let others care for us. We become receivers rather than givers. We submit ourselves to accepting help, advice, and assistance. We let others act for us and in our stead. We may reach the point where others must dress, feed, and change us. This can be hard, even humiliating. But with God's help and good humor, it can be done graciously, in a life-affirming, life-giving manner that will vivify and strengthen our family, friends, and caregivers.

I met George when his wife, Mildred, was a hospice patient. She had Alzheimer's disease. When I visited, she would sing and "dance," her body swaying to a melody in her mind the rest of us could not hear. George, in a wheelchair, had health problems of his own. He also had the most positive, sunny spirit of anyone I've met, despite having faced challenges I could not imagine.

He fought in the Pacific in WWII, and after two solid years of war zone action, hopping from island to island, seeing the majority of his companions killed and witnessing untold horrors, he came home to Mildred a broken man. It took George three years to get over the vivid nightmares, regain the ability to think straight, and have enough strength to plan their future. With faith and sheer force of will he went into business for himself and became successful. They raised a family and experienced some of the postwar prosperity of America.

Then his business burned down. George turned to the insurance company to help him start again, but they called the fire suspicious and never did pay off. Somehow George and Mildred survived, rebuilt their lives, and went on. They had each other, loving children, a spirit of optimism, and Mildred's music. She played the organ in church; and at home around the house she was always singing. At times they had little more than music to carry them through.

When they grew older and more frail, Mildred fought a losing battle with dementia. Before long, the songs in her mind were the only sounds that made sense. George was heartbroken. The two of them had been through so much together, and now she seemed far away. He could touch her, see her, and talk to her, but Mildred was somewhere else. And so it was George in his chair and Mildred swaying back and forth, along with a caregiver who ensured her safety and supported both of them in their final season of life together.

After Mildred died, I continued to visit George. He had been unable to go to church for a long time and asked me for ongoing pastoral support. It was no burden to me. I liked him and was encouraged by him and by how he continued to live with a positive spirit despite his own poor health that kept getting worse, the loss of his wife, and the end of his own life not far off.

For over two years we visited, and George continued to amaze and inspire me. He went through heart problems and surgery during that time. He had painful arthritis and had to give up the idea that he might walk again. His hearing steadily diminished, and the moment came when he could no longer see well enough to use his computer, even though he purchased a large flat screen monitor. It was his lifeline to the outside world, and now he had lost that.

Yet I rarely heard him complain. In fact, when asked, he still went out and spoke from his wheelchair to groups about his military and postwar experiences. His son made it possible for George to go on one of the Honor Flights for WWII veterans to Washington, DC, where George wept with his comrades at the WWII memorial. He showed me the pictures with pride and couldn't stop saying how much that trip had meant to him. He was just such a grateful person.

Whenever George spoke at schools, he found joy in helping young people know and understand their history. Most of all, he simply tried to inspire everyone he met, including his children and grandchildren, his neighbors in the assisted living facility, and me, his chaplain. His message was to always stay positive, never give up, trust God, and keep going. I recall him telling me we could put the plastic surgeons out of business if we just kept smiles on our faces.

One day, George aspirated some food while he was eating and died in his daughter's arms. I officiated his funeral just as I had Mildred's, and words were hard to come by. I continue to see his children once or twice a year and will do so as long as they ask. I could never repay all the gifts George gave me as he lived out the final season of his life.

The gifts some people give live on, sustaining and teaching us each day.

When people consider gifts that they will pass on to others through their death, they may think of a financial inheritance or a business or houses or property. Of course, if God has blessed us with such treasures, it is wonderful to be able to confer wealth and opportunity to the generations that follow. Others may think of leaving mementos or keepsakes to their loved ones, special personal possessions that carry meaning, evoke stories, and remind the living of those who have passed before them.

Material goods are not unimportant, but I wonder if we might think more broadly and deeply than that. When considering the gifts we want to pass on to others, utmost in our minds should be the lessons of life and character that we can share with them through our example and our stories. David Brooks, writing in the *New York Times,* calls this his "moral bucket list," a set of character qualities that consist of what he calls "eulogy virtues."

> It occurred to me that there were two sets of virtues, the résumé virtues and the eulogy virtues. The résumé virtues are the skills you bring to the marketplace. The eulogy virtues are the ones that are talked about at your funeral—whether you were kind, brave, honest or faithful. Were you capable of deep love?

These are the most enduring gifts any of us can bequeath.

Of course, one issue we face when the end of life nears is *regret.* I may feel that I have not been the kind of person I should have been. My moral bucket list may be mostly empty of eulogy virtues. I may have much to confess—words and actions and habits that brought pain to others and that need to be forgiven. Long stretches of my life may not have been exemplary. This does not disqualify us from giving gifts to others in the final season of life. As long is there is life, there is grace to change, to say what should be said, and to make whatever days remain better and brighter than those that have gone before. We need not give up the fight.

I am not being idealistic or unrealistic here. I know it may be impossible to undo what has been done, and others may not believe or accept or want to participate in whatever efforts a dying person puts forth to find redemption. Nevertheless, I believe God will still bless such efforts. If you are in a situation where serious conflict and dysfunction threaten to make the final season of your life just one more period of pain and chaos for you and your family, I urge to you get help and counsel from a minister, chaplain, or counselor so that you can try to find a measure of peace in your final days.

I believe we all have gifts to pass on, gifts that can be enhanced if we take the opportunity to begin sharing them on our walk home at the end of life. It is never too early to start asking the question, "How can I bless those I love through my life and through the season of my dying?"

When I returned to the U.S. from India after my grandmother Annabelle died, I learned more about the circumstances of her death. She had gone to the dining hall at her continuing care facility to eat lunch and had sat down at her usual table with some folks she had befriended. It had become their habit to ask Annabelle to say grace before the meal. They bowed their heads together, and my grandmother was blessing the meal and her friends when her heart stopped beating and she died.

Even at the end, she never stopped giving, and the gift goes on.

## CHAPTER FIVE

# What practices can bring comfort and strength in the final season of my life?

*As it turns out, then, our actual process of moving toward*
*our physical death is much like all of life—daily we learn*
*to die to ourselves so that we might live for God*
*and His glory and for the sake of the world.*

✢ **MARVA J. DAWN**, BEING WELL WHEN WE'RE ILL

THE NIGHT WAS LONG, HIS SLEEP RESTLESS. TWO OR THREE times he reached across the bed to feel her warmth. He reached and reached.

Once, her absence bothered him so much he got up, put on his robe, and walked downstairs. He sat in his chair and listened to himself breathe. An occasional car drove by the house, sending a wave of light across the ceiling. The air was chill. He looked down at his wrinkled hands, blue in the midnight, and saw his wedding ring. Too tired to cry, he sighed, stood up, and trudged to the kitchen.

He grabbed a small glass from a cupboard above the sink and filled it with water. Taking a small sip, he stared out the window on the clear, bright, windless night. Dew shimmered on the grassy lawn where the tree shadows did not reach. He alone saw it while the world slept. The night. The shadows. The glistening grass.

Not that he didn't try to see more. But try as he might, he could not envision her face. Gone so soon? After fifty-five years of seeing each other every day! Every morning, he would arise and go to this very kitchen. He would fix the coffee, turn on the machine, and set out two coffee cups on the counter, one for him and one for her. After retrieving the newspaper, he would go to his chair and read it while the coffee brewed.

Soon, her soft footsteps would sound on the stairs, and he would look up to greet her, precede her into the kitchen, pour out two cups—black—and they would sit at the table together to start the day. As rituals go, it wasn't complicated or profound. Still, he was glad they began most mornings face to face.

How was it, then, that he could not picture her pretty face now? Less than a week after laying her in the ground? Pictures of her were everywhere throughout the house, but he couldn't see them, couldn't see *into* them. He picked them up often and held them in his hands. He leafed through the photo albums of their trips. He traced their life together through them: from the time she was a schoolgirl, to that sexy young mother standing in the yard with a baby on her hip; she who had been the life of so many parties, his dance partner, lover, Valentine; she who had been "mom" on all the Christmases and birthdays and vacations and outings through the years, until the day she became "grandma" and her hair turned white and she was the petite one with sparkling eyes, like dew in the moonlight, in the front row of the large family portrait. He gazed often and hard at this evidence, yet couldn't make sense of it. His vision blurred; his mind fogged; his chest heaved.

Who knows how long he stood there in the night? Out the window, the shadows had shifted, and a wave of weariness crashed over him. He set the glass in the sink and made his way back upstairs. He crawled into bed, pulled the warm, heavy covers up to his chin, and slept for the few hours of darkness that remained.

He awoke as usual, swung his legs over the edge of the bed, put on his slippers, picked his robe off the chair, and tied the belt around his waist. He made his way to the bathroom and performed his morning routine. He ran warm water over his glasses and rubbed them with soapy fingers, washing away the dust and smears. Drying them, he placed them on his nose and looked at the old man in the mirror. He had made it another day.

The morning shone brightly through the living room windows as he went downstairs. Going into the kitchen, he slid open a drawer and separated a new coffee filter from its box. He went to the freezer and retrieved the bag of coffee beans, dumped some into the grinder and then ground them up fine. Measuring out just the right amount, he scooped the fragrant coffee into the filter and placed it carefully in the basket of the pot. He poured the water into the reservoir and closed the top. Reaching up, he grabbed two coffee cups off the shelf and placed them on the counter.

Then he went to retrieve the morning paper.

A simple ritual. A practice. A habit so ingrained that even after his wife's death he instinctively kept putting out two cups for coffee in the morning. You might say this daily practice defined their life together: *they began most mornings face to face.* It marked a regular rendezvous of lovers, life partners, who greeted each other, shared coffee, and started the day off together.

Our practices shape us and our relationships. They not only affect our character and form us as individuals; they also shape the way people will remember us when we're gone.

The practice I described in the story above was a personal, relational practice, a habit developed by a wife and husband that helped make their relationship unique, special, and strong. Maintaining and continuing these kinds of practices with your loved ones, as much as possible, in the final season of your life, can provide great comfort and encouragement.

There are also spiritual practices, disciplines we develop in our relationship with God and the church to make us better representatives of Christ among our neighbors. As you face the final season of your life, I encourage you to think about what practices you might incorporate into your life to strengthen your bonds with God and others. Here are a few of them:

**The practice of life review.** I call this "packing for our journey." As we reach the latter seasons of our life, it is time to reflect, to remember. We look back on our lives and try to make sense of the path we've trod. We come to appreciate things for which we should give thanks. We lament missed opportunities and try to come to peace with our regrets. We consider the people who have filled our lives. Perhaps there are some with whom we should seek reconciliation. Maybe there are others who just need to hear again how much we love them.

One of my important roles as a chaplain is to help people with life review. This is as simple as sitting with them and giving them a safe place in which they can talk about their lives. One person with whom I've sat is named Beverly.

"I had a dream not long ago," she said. "My sister and I were at the roller rink, skating together to that wonderful music. I never did get very good, but she could really skate. In fact, we all saved up and bought her skates, and then later we even got her a case. That was really a big deal, you know, to have your own skates and case."

Beverly told me how the skating rink had been a favorite place for her sister and her to go. How they would scrape up enough change and walk there together. How gliding around the rink on those skates would provide a bit of respite from their hard life at home.

"Daddy drank," she told me, "and would beat the living hell out of my mama. She was little and had long hair and he would grab it from behind and swing her around. He was so mean to her. And sometimes he would come home late at night when the house was locked and pass out on the front porch, peeing all over himself. We were so embarrassed because our friends would see him as they walked to school.

"On Sunday mornings, my sister and I would go to church—any church we could get to—just to get away, because he was drunk every Saturday night. We just wanted out of there. Once I attended a Presbyterian church for awhile and they gave me a free Bible. I still have it upstairs.

"But our favorite thing was to go roller skating."

Tears came to her eyes and she had to turn away. It was the week of Christmas, and I asked about her family. This hard-shelled, funny, coarse, husky-voiced old woman with the wrinkled face and the dark, cluttered house that smelled like stale cigarette smoke grew unusually reflective and quiet. I found myself leaning forward, into her story. She had never opened up and talked so seriously like this before. The change in her demeanor was astounding.

She told how her father ran off to Louisville when she was in her teens. Sometime later a hospital there called and asked her to come and see him and could she help take care of his bill? She didn't go. Her brother was the only one willing, and when he got to the room his own daddy looked up and said, "Who are *you*?"

One time after that he showed up at their house. Mama grabbed a butcher knife and started out of the kitchen after him, but Beverly, pregnant at the time, got between mama and the door and persuaded her not to do it.

Mama never remarried, and every single one of the siblings had been married at least twice. Daddy's drunken doings cast a long shadow.

For years, Beverly, her mama, and her sister were inseparable. But now mama was gone—"for longer than I can remember," Beverly whispered. And sister died a few years back. You could tell losing them was the most profound of all her sorrows. She told me, "I love my kids, I really do. But it's just not the same with them. They didn't go through what we did together."

"In the midst of all that pain," I asked, "do you have some good memories?" That's when she told me about roller skating, and then about the dream. "There we were. We didn't say anything to each other, we just skated. But we were together. And in that dream I felt so peaceful." She turned and looked out the window, wiping an eye with her sleeve.

"You really miss them at Christmas," I said after a moment of silence.

"This time of year is hard, yes," she confessed. "What's that song?—'I'll Be Home for Christmas'—I can't listen to that. There's a bunch of 'em that I have to turn off when they come on."

I wasn't sure what to say.

"But that's enough of my sad story," Beverly said as she slapped her hand on the table.

I'd like to think that conversation helped Beverly pack a few more memories and perspectives in her suitcase as she prepares for her journey.

***The practice of lament prayer.*** The Bible contains many different kinds of prayer and there is one particular form that is most pertinent to someone who is coming to grips with the end of life. It is called "lament," and it involves speaking honestly with God about what you are experiencing and feeling in your sufferings. For example, here is a passage from Psalm 31:

> Be gracious to me, Lord, for I am in distress;
> > affliction is wearing down my eyes,
> > my throat and my insides.
> My life is worn out by sorrow,
> > and my years by sighing.
> My strength fails in my affliction;
> > my bones are wearing down.
> To all my foes I am a thing of scorn,
> > and especially to my neighbors
> > a horror to my friends.
> When they see me in public,
> > they quickly shy away.
> I am forgotten, out of mind like the dead;
> > I am like a worn-out tool
> I hear the whispers of the crowd;
> > terrors are all around me.
> They conspire together against me;
> > they plot to take my life.
> But I trust in you, Lord;
> > I say, "You are my God."

My destiny is in your hands;

 rescue me from my enemies,

 from the hands of my pursuers.

Let your face shine on your servant;

 save me in your mercy.

Do not let me be put to shame,

 for I have called to you, Lord.

⊰ **PSALM 31:10–18**

Note how honest the psalmist is with God as he prays. He does not shy away from expressing his distress, weariness, sorrow, and even his anger and discouragement about his situation and the way other people are treating him. It is not as apparent in this text, but in many of the biblical laments the psalmists also question God: "Where are you?" "How long will I have to endure this?" "I thought you promised to help those who trust you—why aren't you helping me?" At times, the psalmists express feelings of anger and frustration with God and accuse him of forsaking them and hiding himself.

Most of us have been taught that it is not a good thing to complain, especially to God or about God. But the psalms (and other Scriptures) are filled with this kind of praying. It is not "nice" or "religious" in the conventional way we may have been taught about relating to God. But if we take our example from the Bible, we will conclude that God wants us to be honest with him and say directly to him what we are thinking and feeling, even if our words and thoughts are raw and bitter. He's big enough to take that, he won't get angry with us, and we will probably find it will help to get things off our chest.

I recall visiting a Catholic ashram in India for leprosy patients and their families. As we toured the hospital, one of the sisters said to me, "These are the modern-day psalmists." She had heard them cry out to God in their lamentable condition, seeking the comfort of his presence and love in the midst of their sufferings. She encouraged them to do that, and she testified that she had learned a great deal from them about what it means to pray with honesty.

There is one other characteristic of laments that is important to grasp, however. In almost every case, the "complaining" portion of the prayer is part of a *process* that develops through the psalm. Prayers that begin with complaining and bitterness usually end with expressions of faith and praise. In other words, talking things through with God takes time. I'm sure you have had conversations with other people that start in anger, frustration, and conflict but then move toward deeper comprehension and a stronger relationship as you keep talking and listening and trying to understand each other. The same is true in our conversations with God.

The important thing is to pour out what is actually in your heart when you pray. Be honest. If you are angry, say it. If you are confused, don't cover it up with pious phrases. When you feel lost, cry out for help. If you think you're being treated unfairly, complain about it. God is big enough to handle it, and he wants you to trust him enough to let him know what you're truly thinking and feeling.

***The practice of calling the church to pray for us.*** We need others to pray for us as well in this season of life. Presbyterian minister Amy Plantinga Pauw puts it this way: "Those who face death experience the living presence of God through the living presence of the community that cherishes and mourns them" (http://www.practicingourfaith.org/dying-well).

If you are Catholic, that starts with requesting the sacrament of the anointing of the sick. Who should receive this sacrament? The *Catechism* says that the anointing is not only for those who are at the point of death. Whenever someone is seriously ill and death may be on the horizon, it is appropriate to call for the sacrament. The anointing of the sick may be repeated if necessary. It is fitting to call for it before serious surgery, or when an elderly person becomes increasingly frail. You can see why this sacrament is no longer called "extreme unction" or "last rites," to be administered only at the moment of death but may be requested whenever serious illness or debility threatens life. The anointing is a rich resource for Catholics who wish to enlist the support of the church in their time of need.

Other Christian traditions may or may not have specific prayers or rites related to facing the end of life. But if you are associated with a church, I would urge you to request prayer from the minister and congregation at this time. If you have no such affiliation, seek out the hospital chaplain (if an inpatient in treatment) or hospice chaplain (if in hospice care), and they will be happy to pray for you and provide faith support.

***The practice of communicating.*** Nashville country artist Paul Overstreet wrote a song with this important message: "What's going without saying should be said." We take it for granted that our loved ones know we value them, and we think we don't have to put it into words, but "what's going without saying should be said."

What's going without saying *now,* one day won't be able to be said. As we take this walk home together, it is the perfect time to speak. Death brings with it an awful silence.

A few weeks ago, I visited an older man who is in hospice care with only months to live. He and his wife have raised their grandson from when he was an infant, and the boy is now twelve years old. While I was there, he brought out a letter he had written to his grandpa to show me. I had a hard time getting through his heartfelt words of affection for this kind and generous man to whom he looked for nurture and guidance. That little boy said what many of us leave without saying in the final season of life.

Kara Tippetts was a pastor's wife in Colorado who recently died after a long battle with cancer. She wrote a blog of her experiences and a book called *The Hardest Peace.* In my opinion, the most moving (and important) part of the book is her inclusion of three letters, which she appends as a conclusion to her story. There is a letter from Kara to her husband and one to her children. There is also a letter from her husband to the readers, expressing a few thoughts about what they have all been experiencing. This couple was serious about the importance of communicating during the final season of life. They determined to say what many of us might leave unsaid.

One of the most incredible examples of communicating *in extremis* came from Jean-Dominique Bauby, chief editor for French *Elle* magazine, who had a stroke at the age of forty-four and suffered what is called "locked-in syndrome." This is a condition in which the mind is alert, but the person is incapable of movement and speech. He called his condition, "the diving bell and butterfly." His body was trapped, as though within an inflexible deep-sea diving suit, but his imagination was free, like an ethereal winged creature.

Bauby was capable of doing only one thing physically—he could blink his left eye. A therapist came to work with him, and he learned to blink out words from an alphabet board. Remarkably, in ten months, working four hours a day, Bauby composed an entire memoir in which he chronicled his life and experience for others. It is estimated that he made more than 200,000 blinks in "dictating" the book. Jean-Dominique Bauby died just two days after his memoir was published. Even one who could not speak said what many are tempted to leave unsaid.

Our loved ones need to hear our stories, our thoughts, our feelings, our expressions of love and gratitude, even our struggles and doubts during this final season of life. And we need to hear from them as well. Communicating with each other in end-of-life circumstances is not always easy, but I urge you to make it a priority practice.

What's going without saying should be said.

## CHAPTER SIX

# But...I'm afraid

*If not with hope of life,*
*Begin with fear of death:*
*Strive the tremendous life-long strife*
*Breath after breath.*

**⊹ CHRISTINA ROSSETTI**

*I'll make it simple: I don't want to die. I, a Christian,*
*a minister and a person of faith, do not want to die.*
*The thought fills me with fear, and I am ashamed at*
*how little faith I have in the face of what is a universal*
*and uncontrollable human experience.*

*I'll die, no matter how I feel about dying,*
*but I'm not at peace with the reality of death*
*right now, and my fear of death is becoming*

*a more frequent visitor to the dark side of my soul.*
*I've never been a brave person, but bravery*
*isn't the issue anymore. It's acceptance*
*and faith that rests in God, rather than denial,*
*avoidance and the terror of my fears.*

❧ **MICHAEL SPENCER,** "DEATH: THE ROAD THAT MUST BE
TRAVELED" (INTERNET MONK)

JUST BECAUSE A PERSON BELIEVES IN HEAVEN, THAT DOESN'T
mean he's eager to get there.

Michael Spencer was my friend, though only for a short season.
Known as the "Internet Monk," Michael was a pioneering blogger,
writing on spiritual and cultural themes for about eleven years before his untimely death in 2010. You can still read his articles at
www.internetmonk.com.

The Internet Monk was a rare breed. He had a keen mind and
a heart for the kingdom of God. Michael undertook a spiritual
journey that led him away from his Baptist roots into an appreci-
ation of the Great Tradition of historic Christianity. He struggled
in his relationship to the church, but remained faithful as a teacher and campus pastor in an international Christian boarding
school in the hills of eastern Kentucky. He described his quest as
a sojourn through the "post-evangelical wilderness."

Michael was a loving family man and fine teacher with a large
personality. But he had a childlike heart. One characteristic of that
was that Michael had many fears. Perhaps this is not so unusual;
but what set him apart from so many of the rest of us was that he

was honest enough to talk about his fears, even writing about them in the public forum of his blog. Here is an example of his willingness to bare his soul:

> With the arrival of middle age, my fear of death has perched itself on my shoulder like a talking parrot. It waits until every other thought and concern has quieted down, and then it squawks as loudly as possible: "You're going to die, and there's nothing you can do about it." It particularly likes to show up when I am going to sleep at night. I'll say my prayers, begin to doze off, and SQUAWK—"Just a reminder big guy, you're going to die." For a few moments, I live in panic, fear, and despair.

And...

> Call me whatever unspiritual names you like, but I don't want to die. Everything about me wants to be alive in this world. I don't want to say good-bye to my wife, children, and friends. I don't want there to be a last sermon, a last day at home, or a last drive in the country. When someone says we were made for heaven, I say "OK, but that's not the way it seems to me. I appear to be made for living in this body, in this world, and enjoying it." I haven't heard a prospect for heaven yet that sounds better than eating at my favorite barbecue place, making love, or going to the ballpark.

On the one hand, it is refreshing to hear someone voice such honesty, a person so plainspoken about a subject most of us have made taboo. Then again, it can be uncomfortable when it forces us to look in the mirror and recognize that we too have deep fears about death and the process of dying. As for me, I'm right there with Michael Spencer. I am truly not looking forward in any way, shape, or form to hearing that terminal diagnosis and having to face the prospect of my demise. I believe in heaven; I'm just not eager to go through what it takes to get there.

How about you? You are now facing the walk home. I'm sure you have some fears of your own. While we walk together, if you would like to share your fears, anxieties, and doubts and tell me that the idea of going through this final season of life and walking through death's door keeps you up at night, I can relate. If it would help you to say that the prospect of leaving this world and saying goodbye to your family and all that is familiar twists your insides up in knots, making it hard for you to breathe, that you've been too afraid to even talk about this with anyone else, I understand and would be happy to listen.

As I've talked with others about this, I have found it is important to clarify just exactly what you are afraid of. Many folks just know they feel fear, but haven't identified what's causing them to feel that way. It can help to know that, because you may find that comfort and help is closer than you think. So let me start. Maybe if I can tell you some of my fears with regard to death and the process of dying, it can help you discover the source of your own anxieties.

***I am afraid of losing control.*** This guy doesn't like the idea of other people having to take care of him. I have always tried to be a giver and to help others. That has been my vocation, and to think of switching roles so that I'm the care-receiver rather than the caregiver is uncomfortable to me. It's embarrassing, humbling. I don't like the thought of it and probably won't like the reality either.

***I am afraid of the unknown.*** I have taught the Bible my whole adult life and have a pretty good idea of what it says about the afterlife. But I've never been there; have you? No matter how much reassurance my faith, the Bible, the church, and other Christians give me, the fact remains that death involves a step into unfamiliar territory, and I'm leery of that.

***I am afraid of leaving my family, and I am anxious about what will happen to them.*** Yes, I realize I am not indispensable; they will be fine, and God will take care of them. But I will miss them and will miss being an integral part of their lives. Perhaps this goes along with losing control, but I like to think I have a hand in the well-being of my family. When I'm gone, who will fulfill that role?

***I am afraid of pain and suffering.*** This is one of those fears that has actually lessened since I've worked for hospice, for I have seen the remarkable advances in pain and symptom management that are now common in end-of-life care. I tell my patients that it is extremely rare when we will be unable to help someone feel comfortable at the end of life. Nevertheless, I can be kind of a wimp when it comes to pain, and this fear lurks in the back of my mind.

*I am afraid of becoming a dithering, drooling, babbling idiot.* I fear losing my mind. I fear dementia, senility. I fear doing and saying things when I have no idea what's taking place. I fear making my family blush and being the legendary old codger that folks will tell stories about for years. I once made a pastoral visit to a woman after she had suffered a stroke. She was one of the dearest, gentlest, kindest Christian women I've ever known. I doubt she had ever said a cross or crude word in her life. She looked at me and said, "I'm so glad I can still realize what I'm saying. I have always been afraid that one day I'll lose my mind and start going around cussing!" I worry that my fate will be much worse, that I will become the exasperating crazy old man who can't be controlled and who embarrasses those around him every day.

*I am afraid of missing out on life.* There is so much I love in life, so many special events yet to take place in the lives of those I love, so many interesting developments to come in the world that I would love to see happen. If I die, there will still be so many places I won't get to see, so many people I'll miss out on meeting. And besides, the Chicago Cubs have to win a World Series at some point, don't they? If I miss out on that, I'm going to be very upset.

*I am afraid of being a burden on my family and others.* Not only am I concerned about what will happen to my loved ones after I am gone, but I am deeply concerned that the process of my death will be an exhausting, debilitating experience for them.

***I am afraid of being forgotten.*** Think of all the people who have died since the world began. Think of all the cemeteries you have seen over the course of your life. Think of how many obituaries have been written, how many eulogies spoken, how many graves dug and funeral pyres built around the world and throughout time. Now realize that the vast majority of those people simply sank into the dust of history, remembered by few, honored and celebrated by even fewer. Even the names on the tombstones eventually get worn away by the wind and weather. That thought saddens me so much that I feel a deep existential dread when I let myself ponder it.

Have I touched on any of your fears about death or the process of dying?

I have heard patients say that they are afraid of dying alone. They sometimes say they don't want to die in a hospital or nursing home and that they are afraid of being among strangers when they pass. Others would rather not die at home, fearing that the experience might make being in the house difficult for loved ones afterwards. Some folks have particular worries and anxieties related to the afterlife. They struggle to believe in life after death, and they fear an absolute end: becoming nonexistent. Or, they haven't been able to gain a sense of assurance that God will accept them and forgive their sins. They fear judgment, an extended process of purification in Purgatory, or the never-ending fires of hell.

However, most people with whom I deal are more afraid of the process of death than they are of death itself. They have sadness about leaving the world but real fear that it could be a painful, unpleasant, burdensome experience.

Whatever your particular fears or anxieties may be, I encourage you to find someone in whom you have confidence and who is a good listener so that you can talk about your feelings. It may be that the very process of talking them through with a trusted friend or family member will relieve much of your burden. Or, you may find that you require some particular reassurance from a priest or minister about your theological questions, from a medical professional about issues related to pain and symptoms, and from a counselor or social worker about managing your caregiving situation so that doesn't exhaust your family.

I want to assure you that being afraid is nothing to be ashamed of. It is an essential part of being human. Jesus himself wrestled with feelings of great distress in the Garden of Gethsemane, even asking the Father to remove the cup of suffering if it were possible. Earlier that night, when he spoke to his disciples in the upper room about his impending death, he had to infuse his message with continual reassurance: "Do not let your hearts be troubled or afraid" (John 14:27).

Facing the final season of your life is burden enough. Don't take on more by feeling guilty for having fears. Once again, the best answer is for you to get the loving support you need—from God and from those who are there to share his love with you as you take this journey.

**CHAPTER SEVEN**

# Home

*Yet we are courageous, and we would rather
leave the body and go home to the Lord.*

⊹ **2 CORINTHIANS 5:8**

IN ONE OF OUR HOSPITALS WHERE I VISIT PEOPLE WHO NEED
inpatient hospice care, many of these folks go to the floor where
the oncology unit is. The placement of this unit has always been
interesting to me. When you take the elevator up to that floor, the
doors open and you are presented with a choice: the unit to the
right or the unit to the left. To the right, the maternity ward. To
the left, oncology.

To the right, labor and delivery, where new life is brought into
this world.

To the left, a medical unit for serious and life-threatening dis-
eases, where many people leave this world.

Directly ahead of the elevator is a large window, and in front of that window are seating areas for family members and visitors. On some of the sofas and chairs, you see people who are eager with expectation and exhausted, in a good way, from waiting for what they expect will be a glad event. When a baby is born, a little nursery jingle plays over the loudspeakers, announcing the arrival. You can watch small groups going in and out of the maternity ward to see the babies and parents. They emerge with animated joy, sending good news via Facebook and Twitter, calling friends and loved ones, happily celebrating, enthusiastically conversing, sitting back with satisfied smiles. The wait is over. Life has come. It's a new day. Soon, a family will be taking home a new baby.

In some of the other seating areas, the mood is more subdued. Many of these folks are exhausted too, but their tired faces are lined with worry. They have loved ones hanging on at the other end of life, and some of them are not long for this world. This may be the end of a long process or the culmination of a sudden, devastating event. Either way, the slumped shoulders, muted voices, and serious looks tell a much different story.

And as I step off the elevator, it's all right in front of me. The full spectrum of life in miniature, represented by its two termini and those who watch in between.

Sometimes the division is not so clear. At times I've been asked to take a right off the elevator, to go into the unit where celebration is the norm, there to meet the end of life in the place where it was expected to begin. Babies die, and there are few experiences more jarring. On other occasions, I turn left, expecting to say goodbye to someone, only to find revival and renewal of life, a respite from the cold hand of death and a new beginning for someone who had all but lost hope.

But these are the exceptions.

Most days, it's life and vitality to the right, death or debilitation to the left. The beginning and the end. Birth and death.

The faith I hold tells me, in spite of the visible contrasts, that these two places are, in essence, not so different. Both represent life and the prospect of going home.

Birth is the first kind of death a human being experiences. By means of a violent, wrenching process, a baby is forced from familiar surroundings where he or she has been protected, fed, and allowed to grow in comfort. Whatever a baby in the womb actually experiences, that warm place of nurture must feel like home and one might imagine that the last thing the baby would want to do is leave there. But then the little one is forced down the birth canal and into a new world, where a blast of cold air, a blitzkrieg of light and sound, and a breathtaking barrage of sensory stimulation suddenly overwhelms. Life emerges! Life welcomed into this world is, for the baby, life that entails the loss of his or her previous place of existence. From our point of view, the baby is home. From the baby's point of view, home has been lost.

Henri Nouwen once said that the experience of babies might help us contemplate what it is like to die. He imagined twins in a womb debating the question "Is there life after birth?" and suggested that all humans are faced with the same dilemma these babies discussed. We anticipate leaving this place of life and being thrust into the unknown. Our faith teaches us to look forward to seeing the face of God in a realm of glorious light, but we have never been there before. It is this world that is familiar and comfortable. We are loath to leave it.

So, perhaps death may be anticipated as a kind of birth as well. And perhaps the shock of entering our new environment after death will be just as disorienting. But then, as we hope and confess, there will be a Parent to hold, comfort, and feed us. A family to celebrate our arrival. A warm bed in which to rest. A home for us.

To leave the body is to "go home to the Lord."

There are many mysteries about what God has in store for us there. The ultimate Christian hope does not consist of us simply "going to heaven when we die." We will not be "angels" or "spirits" floating around in some ethereal realm. The Bible tells us that one day heaven will come to earth, and earth (the place where humans dwell) and heaven (the place where God dwells) will be one. God will raise the dead to life again, giving us new bodies, and we will live together with him forever in a new creation. The whole world, the entire cosmos, will be made new, and God's will will be done on earth as in heaven. The knowledge of the Lord will cover the earth as the waters cover the sea. The world will be filled with justice and peace. We look forward to an embodied life in a new and better world. Our ultimate home.

The people with whom I work are on a journey to this home. So am I. So are you. We are all concerned about the answer to the question, *"Will God take care of me when I die?"*

When I step off the elevator at the hospital, I have my answer. I look right and see the place of birth, where babies are born and parents take them home. I look left and see the place of death, where the terminally ill experience another kind of birth into a new and better home.

Birth and death. In either case, the way leads home.

## CHAPTER EIGHT

# There is always a day before

My friend Michael Spencer once wrote:

We all live the days before. We are living them now.

There was a day before 9/11.

There was a day before your child told
you she was pregnant.

There was a day before your wife said she'd had enough.

There was a day before your employer said "layoffs."

We are living our days before. We are living them now.

Some of us are doing, for the last time, what we think we will be doing twenty years from now. Some of us are on the verge of a much shorter life, or a very different life, or a life turned upside down. Some of us are preaching our last sermon, making love for the last time, saying "I love you" to our children for the last time in our own home. Some of us are spending our last day without the knowledge of eternal judgment and the reality of God. We are promising tomorrow will be different and tomorrow is not going to give us the chance, because God has a different tomorrow entirely on our schedule. We just don't know it today.

Who am I on this day before I am compelled to be someone else? What am I living for? How am I living out the deepest expression of who I am and what I believe? My life is an accumulation of days lived out of what I believe is true every day.

WWW.INTERNETMONK.COM/ARCHIVE/THERES-ALWAYS-A-DAY-BEFORE

How does it make you feel when you hear this—*"There is always a day before"*?

I hope it doesn't induce paralyzing fear in your heart, mind, and body. The fact that we have a "day before" and perhaps many "days before" can actually energize us to make the most of each day.

I hope it doesn't cause you to change the subject. It is natural to want to try and avoid topics like this until we are forced to face them. However, the "day before" can be a day in which we courageously face all the possibilities of life, even the unpleasant ones, and do what we can and must to prepare for the future.

I hope it strengthens your resolve to live wisely, to prepare as best you can for whatever may come, and to never give up on life, faith, and love.

I hope it helps you to be faithful in doing the small, mundane things that may not seem so important today. Tell your spouse, "I love you." Hug your children. Write that letter you've been meaning to send. Go to church and pray. Have that conversation with your neighbor. Take care of business.

I hope it encourages you to seek God in a fresh way. The Bible says, "So then, whether we live or die, we are the Lord's" (Romans 14:8). God is present to help you on every "day before" as well as on the day when difficult circumstances come calling.

I hope it stimulates you to serve others. Each day is a "day before" for someone, and there are multitudes around us who have run out of them. Who will support them and show them the love that will help in their time of need?

In truth, we only have today.

I saw a cartoon of Charlie Brown and Snoopy sitting on a pier, facing the blue waters of a lake. Charlie Brown says to his dog, "Some day, we will all die, Snoopy!"

Then Snoopy answers, "True. But on all the other days, we will not."

All the other days are the "days before." And they are days for living.

# "How do I be good at dying?"

A FEW YEARS AGO, I RECEIVED THIS EMAIL FROM A FRIEND WHO reads my blog. I had started a series called *"Ask Chaplain Mike,"* and this was the first question I received. I wasn't quite prepared to have to deal with such a serious matter right at the start! But I did my best to answer this friend, and I hope the interchange between us will capture the heart of this book's message for those who find themselves in similar circumstances.

✳

Dear Chaplain Mike,

A neurological illness has ravaged my spinal cord. I live my life in a power chair and lose more ability every day. It has been challenging, but I have always had something I could do in response. I have relearned basic tasks in dozens of different ways, regaining a good measure of independence. I have studied what my elders in the field of disability have accomplished, what tools they used, and what equipment and techniques were available. Then I put in long hours of practice until I could manage the same. Living with a disability is something that one can do well; I've become pretty good at it and have even gained some skill at helping others.

About two years ago, the disease attacking my spine meandered out to have a go at my vagus nerve. In simplest explanation, the combination of progressive motor disability and damage to the nerves controlling my digestive system is slowly starving me. In Paul's words, "the outer man is wasting away," although I can attest that even in this, the inner man is indeed being renewed day by day! I am dying, though undramatically and not so fast I'm ready for my own hospice chaplain just yet. I became aware of the situation last fall, and the lack of options in my complicated situation this past winter.

Having had time to get past many of the emotional

ramifications, I'm currently stuck at this question: *how do I be good at dying?* I am confident in the assurance that Jesus won't suddenly love me less for being cognitively impaired or less capable of outer piety, but I'd still like to run this section of the race well. What does that look like? I feel like I'm wasting precious time, but with my body and mind failing, I can't see any alternative. When you have from six months to two years to live but such little capacity, what do you do besides trying not to burden your family more than necessary?

Dear Friend,

Your e-mail breaks my heart. At the same time, it inspires me. I commend you for the faith and energy with which you have faced your illness and disability. God has blessed you with a spirit of courage and perseverance. As one who has never had to face such trying personal circumstances, I am deeply humbled by your example. Thank you for sharing your story.

As you face the future and what may be your life's final season, I also admire your willingness to ask how you can live it well. I often have to convince people that my job as a hospice chaplain is not to talk primarily about death, but to help people live in the last chapter of their lives.

Life is made up of seasons, or to use another metaphor,

various rooms in a house. We move from room to room, passing through doors that enable us to leave our former surroundings behind as we enter into new settings. We leave our mother's womb and become infants. We leave infancy and learn to toddle. One day, we hug mom and dad goodbye and enter our school years. We graduate from school and move into adult life. We pass through the various stages of adulthood as long as God allows us to live. As we pass through each door, we leave some things behind, and there is grief. But we also find ourselves in a new place, with new things to learn and experience, new dreams that emerge, new goals to consider, new tasks to accomplish.

Some of us, like you, receive the gift of *knowing* that we are in the final season of our lives. This gives us the opportunity, with God's grace and wisdom, to exercise our human capacities for insight, creativity, and action to redeem that season. We know the door that will provide our transition to the next reality—death. But before we pass through that door, there is living to be done.

What would I do as a hospice chaplain coming to visit a person in your circumstances? What counsel would I give you? The first thing I would do is listen and learn. I would try to ascertain what is most important to you. I would learn about your family, your friends, your faith. I would attempt to find out if you have any *unfinished business* that you would like to see taken care of. I would encourage you to think about any *relationships* that you might like to celebrate before you die or, on the other hand, any *unresolved conflicts* you would like to see healed. Do you have any *dreams* you would like to see fulfilled, any *goals* you would like to accomplish? Beyond that, it sounds as though you also have a heart to help others. Perhaps your goals will include ways of using your experience to be a blessing to others in some fashion.

Before I go on, let me make something clear. I'm not necessarily talking about big or grandiose dreams or goals here. Many patients I know realize that some very simple things will make all the difference for themselves and others in their final days.

What *tasks* need to be performed in order to help you and your loved ones face the end of life and take care of the necessary duties that must be performed at that time? Do you have any wishes about the *setting* in which you would like to be during this final season? In your particular situation, it sounds as though you will be dependent upon others at some point. Do you have freedom to choose and work with family, friends, faith community, and others to see that you will have the people you want around you in the place you would like to be? If so, then I would encourage you to talk as much as possible with the important people in your life to make the necessary arrangements.

I would also encourage you not to wait on making a

decision about hospice care, if you think that will be appropriate at some point. Many wait too long to make that choice and fail to realize the benefits of support that hospice can provide. Again, that is because hospice is not just about death; it is about providing support during the final season of life for both patient and those who surround the patient. The question "How can I die well?" cannot simply be answered in a single message, but must be discovered as part of an ongoing conversation with trusted people who care about you.

The Good Shepherd who calls you forth into this experience will go before you, and I am convinced that nothing can ever separate you from his love. Thank you for your trust in sharing your story with me. I hope you will keep me updated as you are able.

Grace and peace,

Chaplain Mike

# Some Practical Considerations

THE MOST IMPORTANT ACTIONS YOU MUST TAKE AS YOU FACE the final season of your life involve making your wishes known through *advance directives* and *adequate practical preparations* so that your loved ones will have the ability to handle your affairs. The following checklist includes some of the key matters you should consider.

## Advance Directives

☐ Have you drawn up a legal *will*?

☐ Have you designated a *Power of Attorney* to handle your financial affairs when you are no longer able to do so?

☐ Do you have a *Living Will* that expresses what you want regarding life-prolonging procedures?

☐ Have you designated a *Health Care Representative* to make medical decisions on your behalf when you are no longer able to do so?

☐ Have you decided about whether you would like to be an *organ or tissue donor*?

Your state may have additional advance directives to consider.

It is important that you discuss your advance directives with your family, your physician and health care providers, and your attorney. Your community may have legal aid assistance programs that can help if you cannot afford a lawyer. You can change or cancel your advance directives at any time as long as you are of sound mind.

Advance directive forms are available from many sources, including attorneys, health care providers, and senior citizen groups. Please be aware that *each state has its own requirements for advance directives* and what they cover. You will want to speak to someone who knows your state's specific rules. Your state government has information available through their website and publications as well.

The best tool I have seen for capturing one's wishes for the final season of your life is called *Five Wishes*. It is published by Aging with Dignity (https://www.agingwithdignity.org/five-wishes. php), an organization that seeks to "affirm and safeguard the human dignity of individuals as they age and to promote better care for those near the end of life." They cite Mother Teresa of Calcutta as their inspirational foundation.

One of the great things about *Five Wishes* is that it is written in plain language and includes *personal* wishes about care and comfort that concern people in the end of life. In forty-two states, *Five Wishes* meets the requirements as a legal advance directive; in the other states, it may be attached to the required forms.

Go to the Aging with Dignity website for more information and to view their materials, or you can contact them at:

Aging with Dignity

P.O. Box 1661

Tallahassee FL 32302-1661

Phone: (850) 681-2010

Toll free: (888) 5WISHES (594-7437)

## Practical Preparations

☐ Does a designated member of your family or your representative know how to access your bank accounts and investments?

☐ Do you have life insurance, company benefits, Social

Security benefits, etc., and does your family or representative know how to access information about that?

☐ Have you discussed with your family or representative what kind of care you would like to receive if and when you are no longer able to care for yourself?

☐ Have you done any funeral planning? Do you know which funeral provider you would like to use, which of their products and services you desire, and what kind of funeral or memorial service you would like to have? Have you spoken with your priest, minister, or pastoral leader about your wishes? Have you shared your wishes with your family?

☐ Have you made arrangements for the disposition of your property and possessions? Your pets?

You may think of other matters that reflect your own personal situation and relationships. What is vital is that you prepare. This will help bring you and those you love peace of mind.

# Of related interest

| Scripture Classics | Scripture Classics |
|---|---|

| **For Everything There Is a Season** | **The Lord Is My Shepherd** |
|---|---|
| *Ecclesiastes 3:1-8* | *Psalm 23* |
| ALICE CAMILLE | MELANNIE SVOBODA, SND |

Alice Camille guides us on a surprisingly modern and personal spiritual exploration of the poem that inspired a popular sixties folk song that became an anthem for world peace. This breathtaking book takes each line of the Old Testament poem and uncovers a powerful message not just for churchgoers, but for anyone seeking answers to questions about life's polarities: planting and plucking up; breaking down and building up; killing and healing; mourning and dancing.

» 104 PAGES | $12.95 | 4" X 6" | 9781627851442

Psalm 23 is one of the most cherished and frequently recited prayers of all times. And it is as relevant for Catholics today as it was when it was first uttered many centuries ago. In the hands of Melannie Svoboda, its words and images take on powerful new meanings about forgiveness, healing, trust and much more. Discover the significance of these green pastures and safe waters in your own life as you prayerfully reflect on each line.

» 104 PAGES | $12.95 | 4" X 6" | 9781627851121